RT &

Authors: Jenni Sorkin & Meredith Tromble
Series Editor: Matthew Koumis
Graphic Design: Rachael Dadd
Printed in England by Offset Colour Print

© **Telos Art Publishing 2002**

Telos Art Publishing
PO Box 125, Winchester
SO23 7UJ England
T   +44 (0) 1962 864546
F   +44 (0) 1962 864727
E   editorial@telos.net
E   sales@telos.net
W   www.arttextiles.com

ISBN 1 902015 34 7 (softback)
ISBN 1 902015. 51 7 (hardback)

A CIP catalogue record for this book
is available from The British Library

Notes
All dimensions are shown in metric and
imperial, height x width x depth.
All work is in private collections unless
otherwise stated.

Artist's Acknowledgements
With special appreciation to California
College of Arts and Crafts for their generous
support of this project.

Special thanks to my husband, Mark
Delepine and my father, Jim Polese for their
early encouragement and support and to
California College of Arts and Crafts for their
support of this project. I want to thank Garth
Fletcher, who generously provided the use
of his JacqCAD Software, and whose
commitment to education and artistic
experimentation is extraordinary. I want to
express my appreciation to Louise Berube
for sharing her expertise and providing a
place and equipment to enable me to
develop my work and to Bethanne Knudson
of the Jacquard Center for her invaluable
technical support. Finally, I would like
to acknowledge Vibeke Vestby, owner of
Digital Weaving Norway, for her vision in
developing a loom that is both
technologically advanced and yet flexible
enough for the individual artist doing
experimental work.

Representation
Lia Cook is represented by Perimeter Gallery
in Chicago, IL, Nancy Margolis Gallery in
New York, NY, and Lew Allen Contemporary
in Santa Fe, NM

front cover illustration
Caress 2001
cotton, rayon/handwoven
33 x 42in (82.5 x 105cm)

back cover illustration
Lia Cook, Studio

portfolio collection
Lia Cook

TELOS

Contents

opposite:
Presence/Absence: In the Folds
Exhibition installation at Miami
University Art Museum
2000
woven cotton & silk

Biography

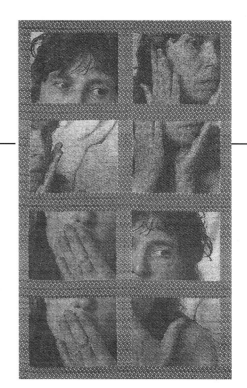

Born   1950, Berkeley, California

Education & Awards

1965, 73	B.A., M.A. University of California, Berkeley
1974, 77,	Fellowships, National Endowment for the Arts
1986, 92	Fellowships, National Endowment for the Arts
1990	Artist's Fellowship Grant, California Arts Council
1993	United States – Mexico Creative Arts' Residency, National Endowment for the Arts
1996	Distinguished Faculty Award, California College of Arts & Crafts
1997	Fellow, American Craft Council
1998	Distinguished Alumnus Award, University of California, CA
2000	Flintridge Foundation Fellowship

Selected Solo Exhibitions

1978, 81, 82, 84,	Allrich Gallery, San Francisco, CA
1980	Renwick Gallery, National Museum of American Art, Washington DC
1980	San Jose Museum of Art, San Jose, CA
1983	Galerie Nationale de la Tapisserie et d'Art Textile, Beauvais, France
1985	'Stage Curtains...Paintings,' B.Z. Wagman Gallery, St. Louis, MO
1987	'Recent Drapery, Miscellaneous Dry Goods and Other High Art', Allrich Gallery, San Francisco
1989	'Crazy Quilts', Galerie Philharmonie, Liege, Belgium
1990	'Lia Cook, Arts in the Academy', National Academy of Sciences, Washington, DC
1993	Ram Gallery, Oslo, Norway
1995	'Lia Cook: Material Allusions', The Oakland Museum, Oakland (tour)
1996	Maureen Littleton Gallery, Washington, DC
1999	'Presence/Absence', Perimeter Gallery, Chicago, IL
2000	Miami University Art Museum, Oxford, OH
2001	'Past Presence', Nancy Margolis Gallery, New York, NY

Selected Group Exhibitions

1973, 75, 77, 89, 92,	
	7th, 8th ,9th, 14th, 15th International Biennial, Musée Cantonal des Beaux Arts, Lausanne
1973	'Anatomy and Fabric', Los Angeles County Museum of Art, Los Angeles
1981	San Francisco Museum of Modern Art, San Francisco, CA
1982	'Jacquard Textiles', Museum of Art, Rhode Island School of Design (tour)
1984	'The Flexible Medium: Art Fabric', National Museum of American Art
1986	'Fiber R/Evolution', Milwaukee Art Museum, Milwaukee, WI
1989, 92	'2nd, 3rd International Textile Competition – Kyoto', Museum of Kyoto, Kyoto, Japan
1990	'The Definitive Contemporary American Quilt', Bernice Steinbaum Gallery, New York, NY
1990	'Heads, Threads and Treads', Santa Barbara Museum of Art, Santa Barbara, CA
1993	'Fascinatie Textiel II', Museum Van Bommel-Van Dam, Venlo, The Netherlands
1993	'California Dreaming', Franklin Parrasch Gallery, New York, NY
1994	'Conversations: Textiles about Textiles', The Textile Museum, Washington, DC
1995	'Conceptual Textiles: Material Meanings', John Michael Kohler Arts Center, Sheboygan, WI
1995	'Starke Falten', Museum Bellerive, Zurich, Switzerland
1997	'Le Biennale du Lin Contemporain', L'Hotel de Sens Bibliotheque, Paris
1998	'Webs:// textiles & new technology', The Design Gallery, UC Davis, CA
2000	'Made in California 1900 - 2000', Los Angeles County Museum of Art, CA
2000	'e-textiles Jacquard 2000', Montreal Museum of Contemporary Art,Quebec
2000	'Remnants of Memory', Asheville Museum, Asheville, NC
2001	'Reality Check – Representational Images in Unlikely Media', The Ohio Craft Museum, Columbus, OH
2001	'Defining Craft 1: Collecting for a New Millennium', Houston Center for Contemporary Craft, TX
2002	'Technology as Catalyst', The Textile Museum, Washington, DC

Selected Public Collections

The Cleveland Museum of Art, Cleveland, OH
Museum Bellerive, Zurich, Switzerland
Det Danske Kunstindustrimuseum, Copenhagen, Denmark
American Craft Museum, New York, NY
Charles A. Wustum Museum of Fine Arts, Racine, WI
De Young Museum, San Francisco, CA
French National Collection of Art, Paris, France
Metropolitan Museum, New York, NY
Milwaukee Art Museum, Milwaukee, WI
Museum of Art, Rhode Island School of Design, Providence, RI
Museum of Modern Art, New York, NY
National Museum of American Art, Smithsonian Institution, Washington DC
Oakland Museum, Oakland, CA

Selected Teaching/Residencies

1976-present   Professor of Art, California College of Arts & Crafts
1990   Artist in Residence, Fondazione Arte della Seta Lisio, Florence
1991   Artist in Residence, Jacquard Project, Muller-Zell, Germany
1995   Artist in Residence, Visiting Artist Jacquard Project, Philadelphia
                College of Textiles & Science

this page: opposite:
Un/mask: Youth   **Small Comforts: Clasp**
2001   2002
woven cotton   woven rayon
75 x 57in (187.5 x 142.5cm)   10 x 13in (25 x 32.5cm)

Selected Publications

1995	*Lia Cook: Material Allusions,* Exhibition Catalogue, Oakland Museum of California, CA
1996	*Fiberarts,* Jan/Feb, 'Lia Cook Revisited: A Radically Fresh Approach to Art Criticism,' essay by Chelsea Miller Goin
1996	*American Craft,* April/May, 'Lia Cook/Material Allusions' essay by Chiori Santiago
1996	*Artweek,* Nov, 'Lia Cook at the Craft & Folk Art Museum' review by Miles Beller
1998	*Conceptual Textiles: Material Meanings,* Alison Ferris, Exhibition Catalogue, John Michael Kohler Arts Center, Sheboygan, WI
1999	*New Art Examiner,* July/August, review by Jenni Sorkin
2000	*Remnants of Memory,* Exhibition Catalogue, Asheville Art Museum
2000	*Textileforum,* Sept, 'Structure & Image,' essay by Lia Cook
2000	*Flintridge Foundation Awards for Visual Artists,* 'Making Sense of Touch,' essay by MeredithTromble, Flintridge Foundation, Pasadena,CA
2001	'The Art of Lia Cook-Presence/Absence: the Digital & the Hand,' Video by Elizabeth Scher, Co-Produced by I.V.Studios & Lia Cook, Berkeley,CA
2002	*Technology as Catalyst,* Catalogue, Textile Museum, Washington DC
2002	*Drapery, Classicism and Barbarism in Visual Culture,* Gen Doy, London /New York I.B.Tauris
2002	*American Craft,* April/May, 'Review: Lia Cook', Sigrid Wortman Weltge

Presence Absence: In The Folds (detail)
1997
woven cotton & rayon

Foreword

by Melissa Leventon

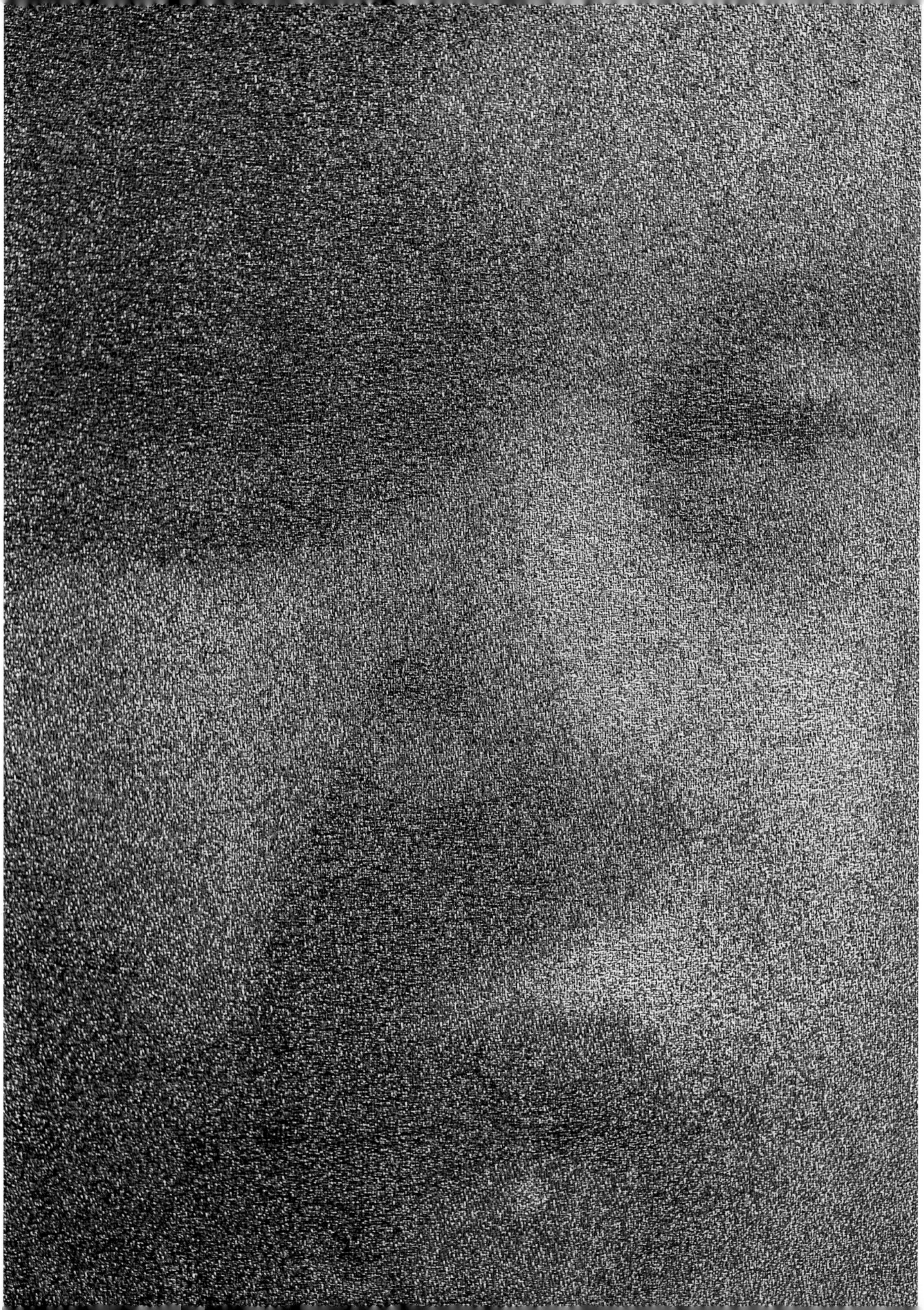

Much of Lia Cook's work over the past twenty years has been driven by drapery, its nature and meaning as subject, object, and metaphor serving as her focus. Drapery became the Cook's-eye view of art, and she used it to confront received art world hierarchies and offer a fresh perspective on familiar things.

Textiles have long been the art world's step-child, but in Cook's topsy-turvy world they are central. Among the conventions that she overturns is the most basic relation between painting and cloth. Canvas has long been used as the silent and invisible substrate for painting but Cook would incorporate a painting cut into narrow strips into her weaving, its imagery fusing with traditional repeating textile motifs. The process turned paintings into their own canvases, swallowing and digesting them into finished works that remained painterly yet were overwhelmingly textile in nature. The process transformed the textiles, too; they were flattened and stiffened like a painter's canvas, and relied on painterly perspective to render three-dimensional effects. In essence, Cook treated painting and weaving as equal partners in the creation of art.

Cook's most recent weavings, which are the subject of this book, exhibit the sensuality and ambiguity, the brilliant sense of color, the large scale and magnification of detail, the love of texture, and the fusion of artistic disciplines, that has long characterized her work. They are as technologically sophisticated and technically rigorous as their predecessors; however they mine fresh ground in several key ways. Gone are the stiff surfaces and meticulously rendered, painterly drapery. Cook's new textiles are invitingly soft and tactile, and many are awash with points of color.

Some are hung draped, but drapery is neither their subject nor their organizing metaphor. Cook's image sources have changed as well, from old master paintings, to family photographs, particularly of the artist herself as both a child and an adult. As a result, the work seems more approachable and more intimate. While it's important that Cook is the subject, this work seems much more about the textures and experience of the human body – the velvety skin of childhood, the signs of age in our hands, the caress of cloth against your cheek – than it is about self-portraiture.

Cook has bravely put herself under the microscope so that we may see ourselves in her image.

Melissa Leventon
formerly Curator-in-Charge of Textiles at the Fine Arts Museum of San Francisco, Principal, Curatrix Group Consultants.

left:
Unmask: Beach Baby
2001
handwoven rayon
64 x 42in (160 x 105cm)

page 14:
Digital Comfort: Backhand
2001
woven rayon
45 x 41in (112 x 102cm)

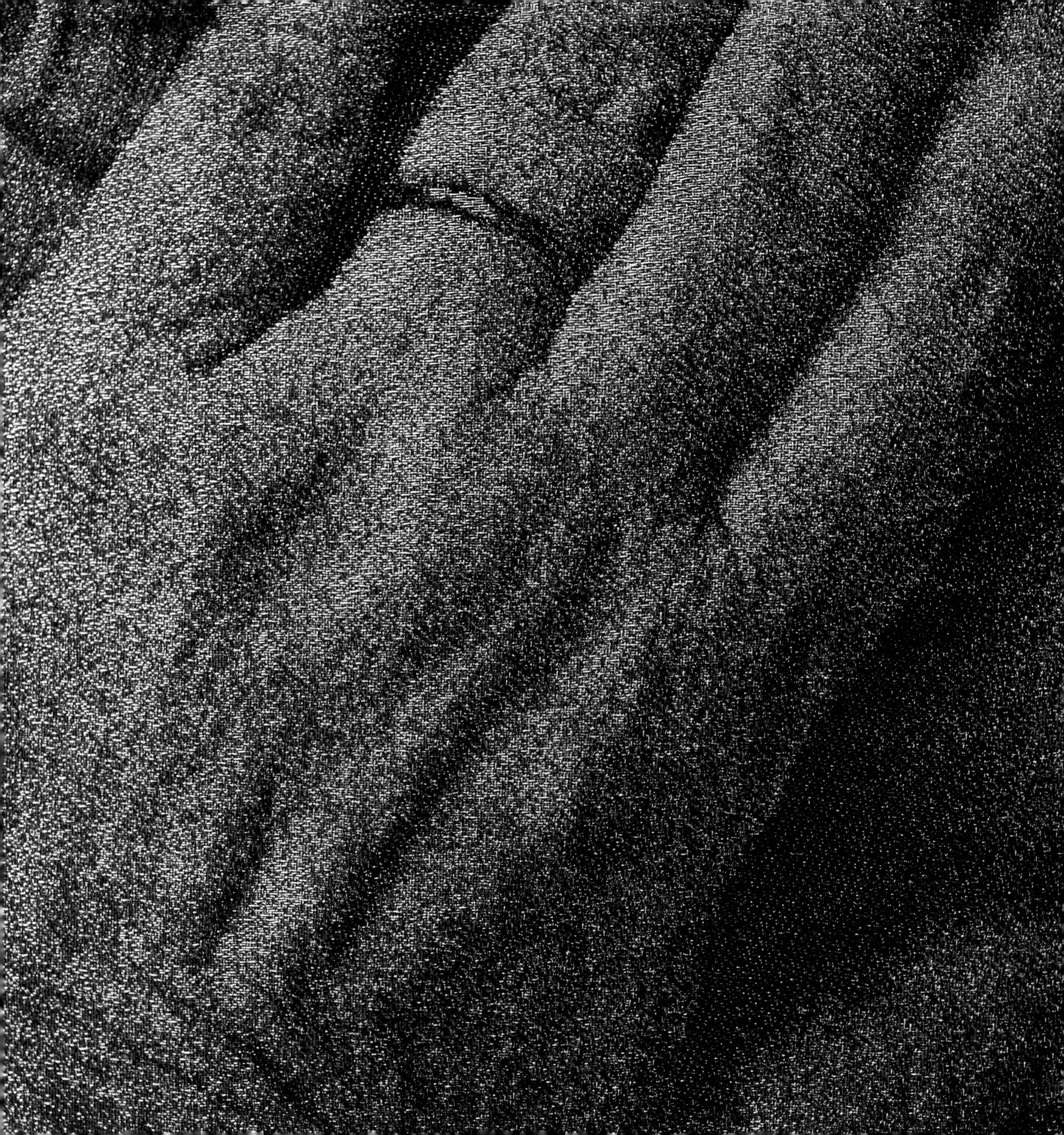

Rapt in Memory:
The Art of Lia Cook

by MeredithTromble

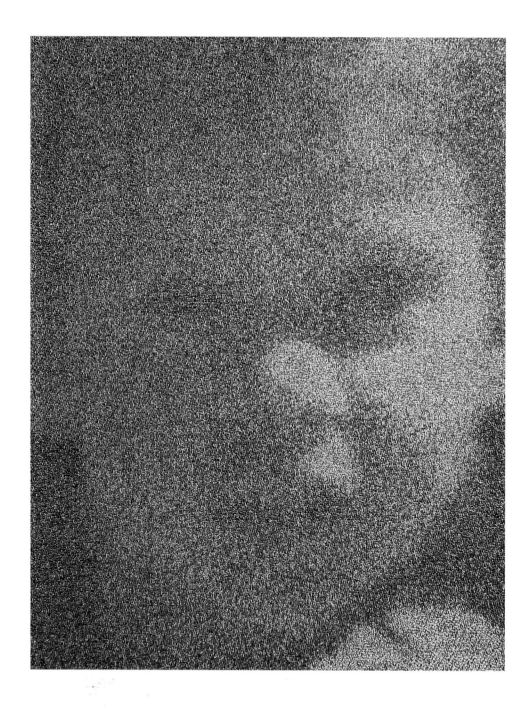

Practicing as an artist in the 'feminine' medium of weaving was an act of radical politics when Lia Cook began her career in the 1970s. For more than thirty years, she challenged the separate and unequal status of weaving in relationship to painting through various and inventive means: Op Art weavings, sculptural weavings, installation weavings, even 'old master' weavings based on the drapery in Renaissance paintings.

Then, after her mother's death in 1996, she came into possession of a trove of family photographs. Her forebears had been settled in California for four generations and her inheritance spanned the history of photography, starting with glass plate prints and daguerreotypes.

Cook, who had been experimenting with photo-based weavings, began to use the family images in her work as a way of extending her art historical references from painting to photography. But these relics of photo history also embodied her personal history. In 1997 she began a series of autobiographical works based on photographs from different times in her life. They raise new questions: why translate an image from photo to fiber, and how does the translation transcend the original? Why weave these particular images? How do the images, fabric or photographic, interact with memory?

Unmask: Basket Baby
2001
woven cotton
55 x 41in (137 x 102cm)

Child – The Frog Princess (2001)

The original photos on which Cook's 'snapshot' weavings are based are, among other things, a medium of social exchange. As they are shared with family and friends they evoke stories. By stirring commentary on the past, they connect people in the present. Looking at snapshots with others is a physical as well as a visual and verbal experience. People reach for them, handle them, touch them. Tellers and listeners bend their heads together, rub shoulders, brush hands, drawing together in the act of looking. Snapshots cue a collaborative exchange of memories; their physical properties – scale, weight, and stiffness – are suited to these transactions.

When Cook transformed family photos into art, she changed the rules of the exchange. Viewers of art images, in modern Western culture, play by different rules than viewers

of snapshots. They stand at a respectful distance, they display more formal postures and gestures, they most definitely do not touch the images. These images could not be passed from hand to hand, anyway. Their pictorial qualities would dissolve as their soft body responded to the grasp by folding and draping. But even as the image disintegrated into folds, they would wrap the touching hands in texture and warmth. That promise of enfoldment suggests a different stage in memory exchange – the moments after looking at the snapshots. The mind returns to the present, the images fade from the mind's eye, but the pleasure (or pain) of the emotional exchange lingers as a mood, a subtle, enveloping sensation. These snapshot 'translations' offer a material metaphor for this experience, for which English has no name.

This promise of a sensual experience is just that – a promise – however, because of the position of the weavings as 'art'. There is a contradiction between the inviting substance of the cloth and the ways we are permitted to interact with it. This enforced distance is a necessary condition if the works are to deliver their emotional freight. It separates us from our habits of looking, and makes the images strange; it gives us time to understand that we are not looking at these images for their narratives, but looking beyond them towards something invisible, the action of memory.

This is not to say that the specific stories are incidental to the work. Cook has chosen sources that fold seamlessly into her larger themes. Her impression of the frog costume was taken in the dark, from the inside. It was not a visual but a touch memory. The weaving made decades later may be more suggestive of the truth of her memory than the snapshot taken at the time. We look through the image towards something 'visible' not to our eyes, but to our skin.

I remember being in that frog costume, the feeling of being totally enclosed by that fabric. It was an important memory for me.

The Frog Princess
2001
woven tencil & rayon
125 x 41in (312 x 102cm)

At first you look at Babe and you think it's printed. As you get closer you realize the image is constructed, actually made of threads. It's physical; it could be experienced through your skin.

Sensuality is always in my work, whether it is in the fabric or on it. Fabric is something we don't notice very much, but it's a very sensual thing. We sleep on it, we are covered with it. It is always on our bodies.

Snapshot: Babe
2000
woven cotton & rayon
30 x 42in (75 x 105cm)

Maiden – Snapshot: Babe (2000)

"Touch is as much subject to the kinds of disturbance we might more readily associate with sight, and to the kinds of 'double claim on sight and the act of seeing that Freud described as exerting pressure on the subject from both conscious and unconscious sources."

Briony Fer [1]

Cook's predilection for the pleasures of touch is what made her a weaver. Haptic concerns characterize her work, from the rippling, three-dimensional weave in 'Stepping Down' (1981) to references to fabrics handled in daily life such as 'Hanging Net' (1984),'Through the Curtain' and 'Up from the Sea' (1985) and 'Leonardo's Quilt' (1990), to the commentary on the sexual politics of touch which is central to the 'Point of Touch' series.

As with 'The Frog Princess' and 'Girl with Elephant' the snapshot that became 'Babe' carries a memory soaked in touch. Intimate, carefree, the young Cook smiles an invitation over her shoulder. She appears to be lying on her stomach. Looking at the image, we might imagine our own skin pressed full length into the earth, relaxed in gravity's embrace.

"At first you look at 'Babe' and you think it's printed," says Cook. "As you get closer you realize the image is constructed, actually made of threads. It's physical; it could be experienced through your skin. Sensuality is always in my work, whether it is in the fabric or on it. Fabric is something we don't notice very much, but it's a very sensual thing. We sleep on it, we are covered with it. It is always on our bodies." The sensual quality of Cook's photographic weavings stands out particularly when they are compared to similar photorealist paintings, such as Robert Bechtle's 'Untitled' (Bechtle and Family) (1972).

"Photorealists," according to an Oakland Museum brochure for Bechtle's retrospective, "base their works on photographs, using such mechanical means as copying onto a grid or projecting the image onto the canvas to transfer the information. The finished work is made to appear photographic, with even tones, flattened forms, and apparently unselective detail." [2]

Point for point, 'Babe' qualifies – based on photographs, information transferred by mechanical means, and photographic appearance – except for the 'canvas'. In these works, Cook stands in relation to photorealist painting as Eva Hesse stood in relation to minimalist sculpture, subverting the cool, hard, purity of the style by executing it in flexible, responsive materials. Just as Hesse's version of the minimalist cube, 'Accession I' (1967) practically begs the viewer to reach in and touch the interior, 'Babe' lures the viewer towards a closer, physical acquaintance.

Big Girl With Elephant
2002
woven cotton
240 x 54in (600 x 135cm)

Woman – Presence/Absence: Gather

Identity, according to the philosopher Hilde Lindemann Nelson, is a complex narrative consisting of a fluid interaction of the many stories surrounding the things that seem most important about you, from your own point of view and the point of view of others, over time.[4] For, in many ways, Cook's photographic weavings are just such a narrative of identity, incorporating views that others held of her with her own views of herself over time. She imbues her past with meaning in light of her present, identifying and reinforcing the things that seem important to her, re-weaving them into her life.

But there is a significant difference in the 'Presence/Absence' series, which Cook began in 1997. Her body is still in front of the camera, but now she is also the photographer. The family and friends implied in the snapshot series are gone, along with the time of which they were a part. She records her mature appearance with a digital camera, alone. In the completed woven image, cloth and skin echo each other.

"It remains true for us that hunger is the best spice, and intense sensual pleasure, like gratitude, is the opposite of taking for granted."
Noelle Oxenhandler [3]

left:
Presence/Absence: Gather
1998
woven cotton & rayon
48 x 48in (120 x 120cm)

above:
Presence/Absence: Fur
1999
woven cotton & rayon
51 x 47in (127 x 117cm)

For example, in 'Presence/Absence: Gather', the gently draped cloth repeats the rounding of her abdomen. At other times, the wrinkling cloth rearranges the depicted wrinkles on her face.

The moments preserved in 'Presence/Absence' differ from the snapshot moments because they are not occasions; they are significant simply because Cook is alive. They show transitions – she is thinking, turning, touching, twisting, moving, full of life. Yet the underlying movement of the piece speaks of her potential absence: the rippling cloth distorts and conceals her image. In these works, Cook contemplates not her story, but her existence. She no longer takes it for granted, but, rapt in memory, looks beyond her story to her silence.

Following her gaze, we confront our own final quiet.

1.   Briony Fer, from *The Work of Salvage: Eva Hesse's Latex Works*, Eva Hesse [ed. Elizabeth Sussman], San Francisco Museum of Modern Art, San Francisco and Yale University Press, New Haven, 2002 p. 93.

2.   Robert Bechtle, *California Classic: Realist Paintings*, Oakland Museum (exhibition brochure, 2000), http://www.museumca.org/exhibit/exhib_bechtle.html

3.   Noelle Oxenhandler, *Fall from Grace: How modern life has made waiting a desperate act*, New Yorker, June 16, 1997, p. 68.

4.   Hilde Lindemann Nelson, *Damaged Identities: Narrative Repair*, Cornell University Press, Ithaca and London, 2001, p. 7.

Presence/Absence: Glimpses
1998
woven cotton, silk & linen
63 x 38in (157 x 95cm)

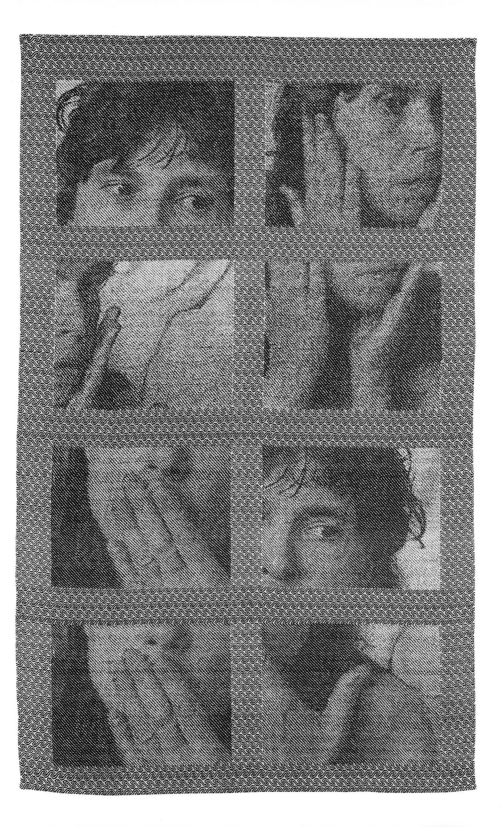

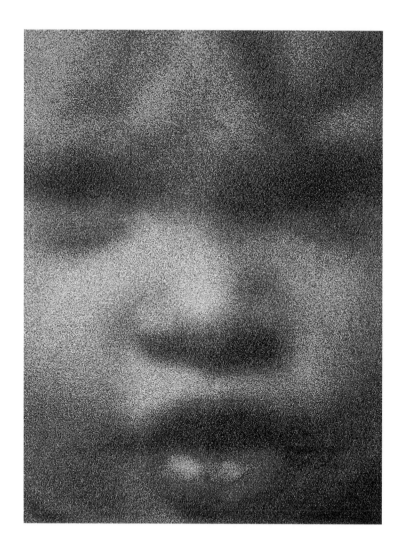

Traces: Intent
2002
woven cotton
72 x 55in (180 x 137cm)

Weaving Possession

by Jenni Sorkin

For the last 30 years, Lia Cook has both defined and defied the limits of weaving, expanding the borders of fiber-based art production. Achieving international recognition at an early age, Cook's career has been marked by her extraordinary technical abilities, origination, and innovative use of advanced techniques.

In 1973, newly graduated from the University of California, Berkeley, Cook was included in the 6th Lausanne Biennial, a prestigious international tapestry exhibition held in Switzerland that showcased cutting edge fiber-based production. Cook's inclusion led to early recognition within the international fiber community, and invitations to participate in the 7th and 8th Biennials (1975, 1977). Back at home, Cook received two of her four National Endowment for the Arts fellowships (1974,1977,1986,1992), before the age of 35.

Computer generated but hand-woven, Cook's structures are distinguished by their highly reflective, nuanced surfaces, where the woven image is twice-determined; her textiles utilize thousands of colored threads to create an image, overlapping layers of patterns to build a repeating, textured surface through weaving.

This process results in a photographic or painted image embedded directly into cloth that is hung freely from wall, rather than flattened and framed. Hand looms and computers are inextricably linked technologies. One intersection of warp and weft in weaving is the computer pixel's earliest ancestor; early loom technology has a very strong relationship to early computer technology. In use by the beginning of the 19th century, Jacquard looms used a punch-card system to program complex patterns that were woven manually. This system was subsequently adapted for use in early computing machines. Using digital technology, Cook weaves manually on a recently developed digital Jacquard hand loom.

Individual units become fuzzy or diffused when viewed in close proximity, both woven threads and pixels embody the entire spectrum of color needed to create the intensity and realism of a richly detailed image. Clicking to enlarge images beyond recognition now seems like second nature, but museum-goers still marvel at the intricacies of George Seurat's pointilist paintings, where figuration is achieved through thousands of colored dots. Art and technology have a historically intimate relationship; it is no surprise that such a moment in painting arose at the height of the industrial revolution in late 19th-century France.

In addition to her substantive and groundbreaking computer-based processes, Cook has continually explored under-utilized and outmoded technologies in relation to contemporary art, such as the aforementioned Jacquard loom and the re-creation of historical silk patterns. Her commitment to broadening the conceptual and formal concerns of woven structures has infinitely expanded the definitions of what weaving is, and what it can do.

Beginning in the late 1960s, Cook was an active participant in the vibrant Bay Area art community, experimenting independently before attending graduate school in the early 1970s. With the feminist movement still a recent phenomenon, artists all over the country facilitated its rapid development, organizing groups and meetings to aid and enrich their art practice. Likewise, Cook joined an all-women group of artists committed to fiber-based practice, providing a supportive, stimulating environment in which to share work, and exchange ideas and technical information. While craft was crucial to the identity and concerns of the 1970s Bay Area art scene, San Francisco maintained a separate and distinct art world, where photography and painting dominated the galleries, and performance was the cutting-edge medium shown in the city's legendary alternative venues. In 1975, she joined the faculty of the California College of Arts and Crafts in Oakland, where she is still currently Professor of Art.

The Frog Princess (detail, see also p19)
2001
woven tencil & rayon
125 x 41in (312 x 102.5cm)

overleaf:
Material Pleasures
1993-1997
Installation, woven cotton & rayon
192 x 384in (480 x 960cm)

Given her range of technical expertise, Cook has brought a previously unseen intensity and depth to her image making, incorporating other mediums, such as painting, video, and photography, into her loom-based production. Beginning in the mid-1980s, Cook came to utilize cloth not just as a material process, but also as a subject matter. Her 'Crazy Quilt' series examined the material history and American tradition of patchwork, or 'crazy' quilts, sewn piecemeal from domestic scrap fabrics by women. Creating a dizzy collage of pattern and density within a singular composition, Cook wove, rather than sewed, quilts, eradicating the barriers and biases of form, merging American quilting traditions with the one-thousand year history of European woven tapestries.

In 1990, Cook embarked on a ten-year historical project in the course of three distinct bodies of work, mining Renaissance paintings for their lush draperies, gowns, and decorative fabrics. The 'New Master Draperies' (1990-1992) series focuses on the domestic fabrics found within the backgrounds of paintings by Michelangelo, Leonardo Da Vinci, and Artemisia Gentileschi.

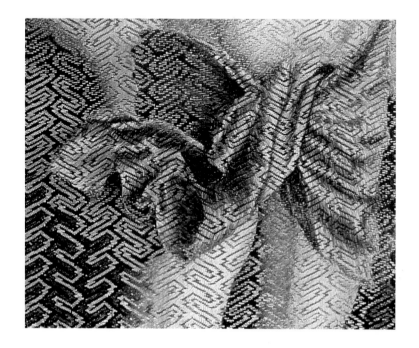

Loin Cloth: Anonymous (detail)
1995
pressed linen, rayon, acrylics & dyes
52.8 x 65in (132 x 164cm)

opposite:
Point of Touch: Intention/Contention
1996
woven pressed linen, rayon & oils
51 x 60in (127 x 150cm)
in the collection of the M. H. De Young
Memorial Museum, San Francisco

By making their details the centerpiece of her works, cloth is illuminated as a sculptural form unto itself. Cook's series functions as a critique of the art-craft hierarchy established during the Enlightenment, where painting and sculpture were privileged as intellectual labor, while utilitarian crafts such as pottery and weaving were viewed as physical drudgery. Cook redistributes the mind-body division in visual terms, reclaiming the legacy of the anonymous women weavers.

Cook completed two additional bodies of work using Old Master painting, the 'Loin Cloth' (1995-1996) and 'Point of Touch' (1995-1997) series.

Partially influenced by Leo Steinberg's provocative history, 'The Sexuality of Christ' (1983), the 'Loin Cloth' series examined male sexuality by appropriating fragmented images of men below the waist, concealing or revealing the genitalia. Conversely, 'Point of Touch' focused on the connection between sensual clothing and female sexuality.

In 1997, Cook began a series of self-portraits known as 'Presence/Absence', weaving directly from video imagery. 'Glimpses II' (1998) is a black and white weaving broken into eight grids, carving up the body: a slice of face, one shoulder, hand over mouth, eyes wide and alert. Through frozen frames, Cook enacts her own mute drama of self-surveillance. Her work of the last two years continues on this trajectory, growing larger in scale and more saturated in color. There is an urgency in her series 'Traces: in Fracture' (2001), one mouth is repeated vertically over and over and over again in a lush frenzy of pink, the white teeth and cavern of nostrils working to twist the mouth into an expression of near pain, alluding to a physical injury or emotional state. 'Traces: Big Beach Baby' (2001) is a massive blow-up of a childhood-era color photograph of the artist. What appears as innocent in a photo album or a small frame atop the mantel becomes overwhelming and disturbing in its mural-sized, woven incarnation. Over 13-feet

long, such a form becomes sculptural, a curtain unfurling in the middle of the room. Much in the vein of Claes Oldenburg's oversized food sculptures, baby pictures exude a bland cheerfulness, mawkish and sentimental until they are made unnecessarily, unnervingly gigantic.

Cook's title 'Trace' necessitates a closer reading of what is known as the index, the human vestiges such as footprints or shadows, that temporarily record the body's physicality. Cloth is an index, retaining the memory of the body even in its inertia, holding the creases and contours of its wearer; likewise, photography is also an index, recording what Allan Sekula terms the 'possessive individualism' found within portraiture. Through the reweaving of her photographic archive, Cook asserts the contingency of ownership, attempting to regain possession and occupy the space of a memory that often belongs to someone else, framed by a parent or relative either through the snapshot, or in its accompanying narrative.

Unmask: Youth
2001
woven cotton
75 x 57in (187 x 142cm)

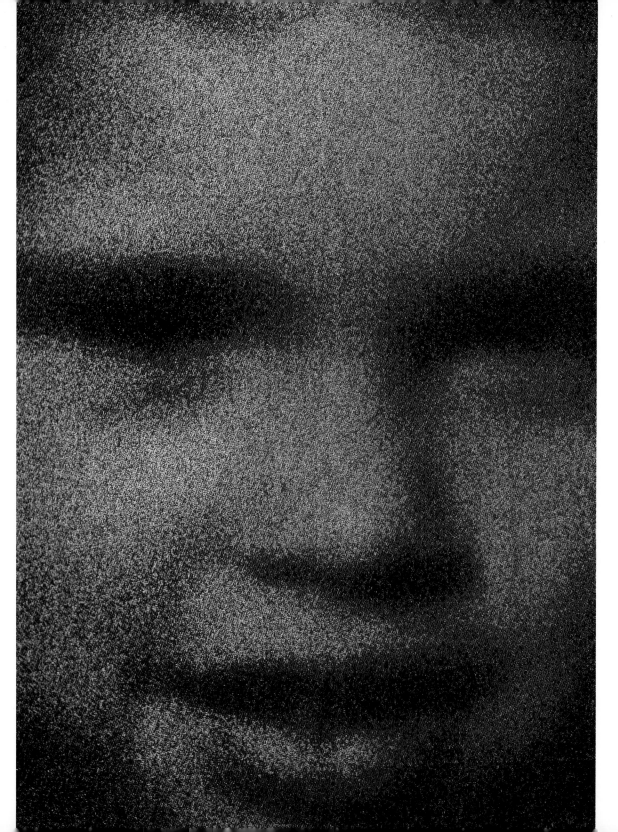

Familiar but unrecognizable, Cook's woven photographs create unexpected moments of sensual recognition, without any specific source of memory, like watching, riveted, someone else's home movie. Translucent, haunting, and filmic, her weavings loom large, barely breathing, pinned to the wall like so many butterflies. Their enormous scale, however, transcends the inherent fragility of cloth, creating the feeling of a projected image.

Both weaving and photography explore the materiality of light, harnessing and infusing compositions with gossamer moments: metallic threads, shiny satin weaves, specific lenses papers, and using available sources of light to shoot or develop film, are all deliberate methods of creating or controlling shimmer and glare. Cook's light is seductive and moody.

Ostensibly woven from a black and white photograph, 'Big Baby' (2000), radiates the familiar blues and grays that often accompany black and white imagery – the navy blacks and steely whites that blur and smudge the contours of Cook's childhood body. Such an image glows with the faint intimacy of old movies one watches in darkened rooms on late-night TV screens with the volume turned low. The voices are muffled, and we lean forward, straining to hear. We are lost in someone else's story.

Lia Cook has infused her weavings with the narrative potential of film. Rather than waiting for the curtains to make their way to the edges of the screen, she has crept into the projector booth and started the film, altering the materiality of the cinematic image, and how we experience it. Caught in her shimmering drama, we are in the grip of Now.

Jenni Sorkin
Freelance critic
Research Assistant,
The Museum of Contemporary Art,
Los Angeles.

Traces: Fracture
2001
woven cotton & rayon
105 x 56in (262 x 140cm)

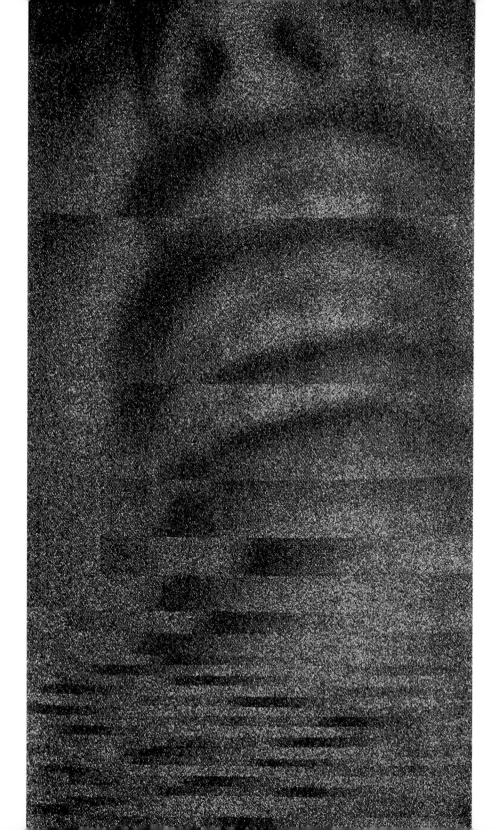

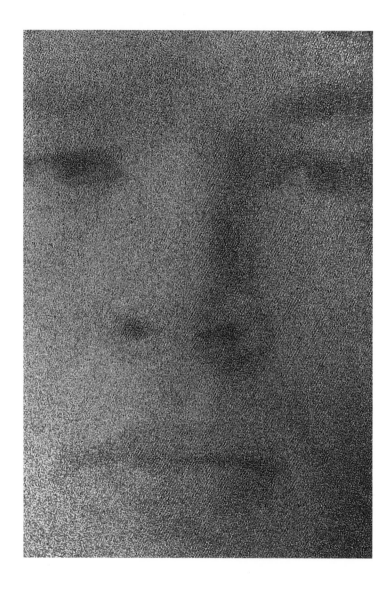

above:

Traces: Young Man
2001
woven rayon
61 x 41in (152 x 102cm)

opposite:

Hands On Spots
1999
woven cotton & silk
91 x 78in (227 x 195cm)

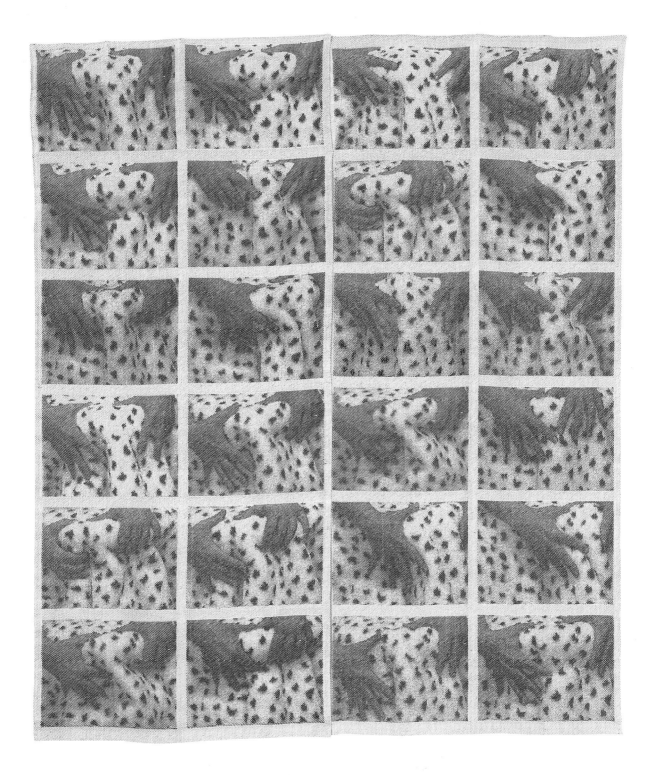

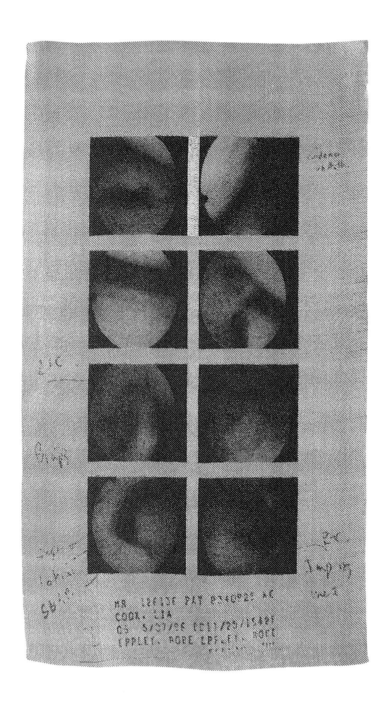

left:
Micro/Macro: Evidence
1999
woven cotton & rayon
71 x 41in (177 x 102cm)

right:
Presence/Absence: Self-Portrait
1997
woven cotton & rayon
(video still)
34 x 20in (85 x 50cm)

Small Comforts: Digit
2002
woven cotton & rayon
8 x 8in (20 x 20cm)

opposite:
Digital Comfort: stretch
2001
handwoven cotton & rayon
36 x 47in (90 x 117cm)

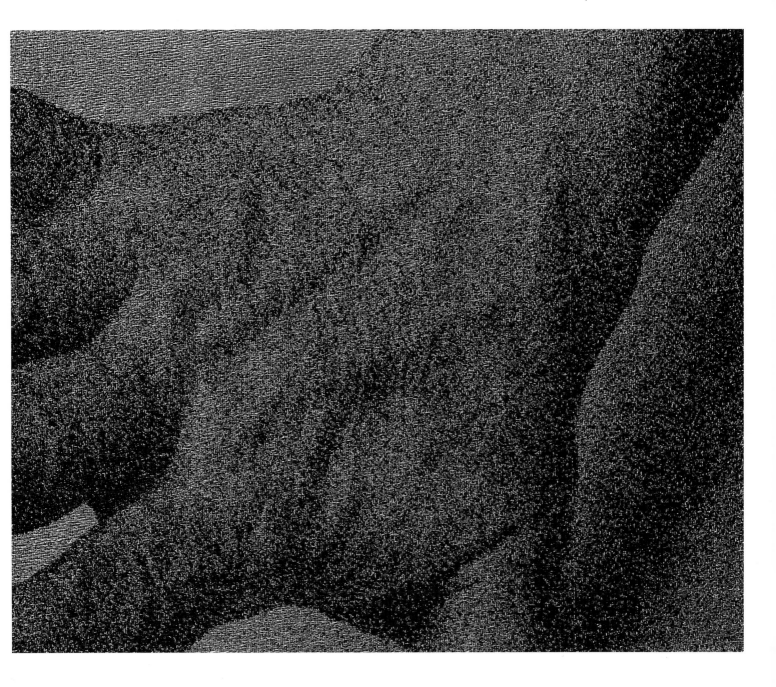

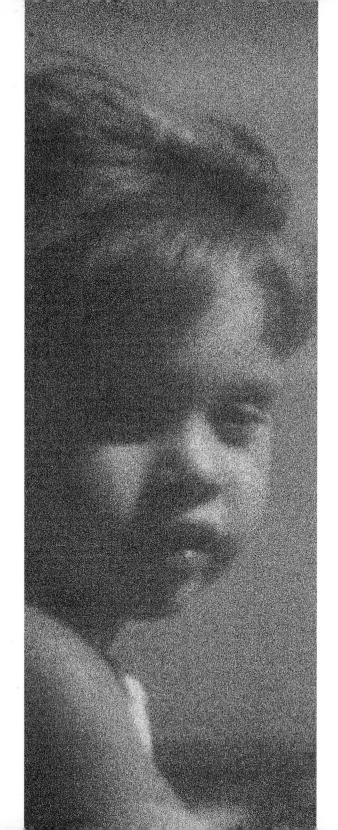

this page:
Traces: Big Beach Baby
2001
woven cotton
160 x 56in (400 x 140cm)

far right:
Traces: Wonder
2002
woven rayon
77 x 41in (192 x 102cm)

Other titles in this series

Vol 6: Anne Wilson
By Tim Porges and Hattie Gordon
ISBN 1 902015 22 3 (softback)

Vol 8: Helen Lancaster
ISBN 1 902015 29 0 (softback)
ISBN 1 902015 45 2 (hardback)

Vol 9: Kay Lawrence
ISBN 1 902015 28 2 (softback)
ISBN 1 902015 44 4 (hardback)

Vol 10: Joan Livingstone
ISBN 1 902015 27 4 (softback)
ISBN 1 902015 43 6 (hardback)

Vol 11: Marian Smit
ISBN 1 902015 32 0 (softback)
ISBN 1 902015 46 0 (hardback)

Vol 12: Tanaka Chiyoko
ISBN 1 902015 24 X (softback)
ISBN 1 902015 42 8 (hardback)

Vol 14: Lia Cook (Sept 02)
ISBN 1 902015 34 7 (softback)
ISBN 1 902015 51 7 (hardback)

Vol 15: Jane Lackey (Sept 02)
ISBN 1 902015 35 5 (softback)
ISBN 1 902015 52 5 (hardback)

Vol 16: Gerhardt Knodel (Sept 02)
ISBN 1 902015 47 9 (softback)
ISBN 1 902015 48 7 (hardback)

Vol 17: Kyoung Ae Cho (Feb 03)
ISBN 1 902015 35 5 (softback)
ISBN 1 902015 50 9 (hardback)

Vol 18: Jason Pollen (Feb 03)
ISBN 1 902015 73 8 (softback)
ISBN 1 902015 74 6 (hardback)

Vol 19: Barbara Layne (Feb 03)
ISBN 1 902015 36 3 (softback)
ISBN 1 902015 76 2 (hardback)

Vol 20: Kay Sekimachi (Feb 03)
ISBN 1 902015 77 0 (softback)
ISBN 1 902015 78 9 (hardback)

Vol 21: Emily DuBois (Feb 03)
ISBN 1 902015 38 X (softback)
ISBN 1 902015 54 1 (hardback)

Vol 22: Gyöngy Laky (Feb 03)
ISBN 1 902015 39 8 (softback)
ISBN 1 902015 56 8 (hardback)

Vol 23: Virginia Davis (Feb 03)
ISBN 1 902015 40 1 (softback)
ISBN 1 902015 57 6 (hardback)

Vol 24: Piper Shepard (Feb 03)
ISBN 1 902015 81 9 (softback)
ISBN 1 902015 82 7 (hardback)

Vol 25: Valerie Kirk (Feb 03)
ISBN 1 902015 37 1 (softback)
ISBN 1 902015 55 X (hardback)

Vol 26: Annet Couwenberg (Feb 03)
ISBN 1 902015 79 7 (softback)
ISBN 1 902015 80 0 (hardback)

Vol 27: Susan Lordi Marker (Feb 03)
ISBN 1 902015 41 X (softback)
ISBN 1 902015 58 4 (hardback)

Vol 28: Agano Machiko (Feb 03)
ISBN 1 902015 59 2 (softback)
ISBN 1 902015 60 6 (hardback)

Vol 29: Fukumoto Shihoko (Feb 03)
ISBN 1 902015 61 4 (softback)
ISBN 1 902015 62 2 (hardback)

Vol 30: Cynthia Schira (Feb 03)
ISBN 1 902015 63 0 (softback)
ISBN 1 902015 64 9 (hardback)

Vol 31: Kumai Kyoko (Sept 03)
ISBN 1 902015 65 7 (softback)
ISBN 1 902015 66 5 (hardback)

Vol 32: Suzie Brandt (Sept 03)
ISBN 1 902015 67 3 (softback)
ISBN 1 902015 68 1 (hardback)

Vol 33: Darrel Morris (Sept 03)
ISBN 1 902015 69 X (softback)
ISBN 1 902015 70 3 (hardback)

Vol 34: Pauline Burbidge (Feb 04)
ISBN 1 902015 71 1 (softback)
ISBN 1 902015 72 X (hardback)

Visit www.telos.net for further details